GOODNIGHT HOUSTON

WRITTEN BY JENNIFER AND KYLE SOLAK • ILLUSTRATED BY PAUL DOLAN

AMP&RSAND, INC.

Chicago • New Orleans

ISBN 978-1450706230

Design
David Robson, Robson Design

Published by
AMPERSAND, INC.
1050 North State Street
Chicago, Illinois 60610

———————

203 Finland Place
New Orleans, Louisiana 70131

———————

www.ampersandworks.com

———————

See the acknowledgments page at the back
of the book for additional credits.

———————

www.GoodnightHouston.com

———————

Printed in China

10 9 8 7 6

To our sons, Garrett and Elliott.
We wrote this book to introduce them to this wonderful city
and hope it will inspire all kids and parents
to explore the fun to be had in Houston!

The stars at night are big and bright,
In Houston, it's time to say goodnight.

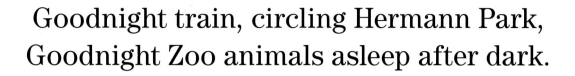

Goodnight train, circling Hermann Park,
Goodnight Zoo animals asleep after dark.

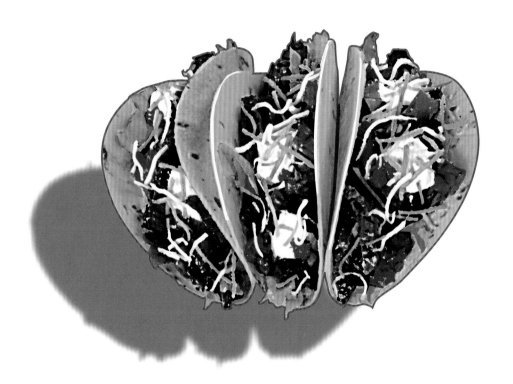

Goodnight spicy tacos and juicy barbeque,

Goodnight Children's Museum, goodnight Buffalo Bayou.

Goodnight to the artists and their funky art cars,
Goodnight Miller Outdoor Theatre, under the stars.

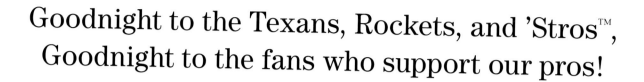

Goodnight to the Texans, Rockets, and 'Stros™,
Goodnight to the fans who support our pros!

Goodnight Theater District and the stories you tell,
Goodnight wildcatters, goodnight oil wells.

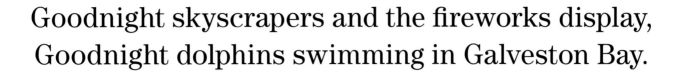

Goodnight skyscrapers and the fireworks display,
Goodnight dolphins swimming in Galveston Bay.

Goodnight Shipley Do-Nuts and the House of Pies,
Goodnight to astronauts, commanding the skies.

Goodnight Arboretum and those beautiful trees,
Goodnight Aquarium and life from the seas.

Goodnight brave cowboys in the Rodeo,

Goodnight Presidents' heads, goodnight Orange Show.

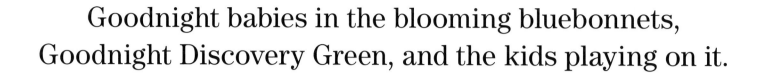

Goodnight babies in the blooming bluebonnets,
Goodnight Discovery Green, and the kids playing on it.

Goodnight ice skaters and the Waterwall rushing down,

Goodnight special city, my very own H-town!

Howdy, Houston!

The **Sam Houston Monument**, located in Hermann Park, shows Texan hero and statesman, General Sam Houston, leading his men into the battle of San Jacinto. The sculpture is positioned to point towards the site of the battle.

Kids have been riding the **Hermann Park Railroad** around Hermann Park for more than 50 years!

Set in a lush 55-acre tropical landscape, the **Houston Zoo** is located in beautiful Hermann Park and is home to more than 6,000 animals representing more than 800 species.

In Houston, **tacos**, a Tex-Mex classic, and **barbeque**, a slow-cooked Texas delicacy, are favorite foods.

Since 1980, The **Children's Museum of Houston** has been dedicated to transforming communities through innovative, child-centered learning. It is a "Playground for Your Mind™". Can your mind come out to play?

Buffalo Bayou is the main waterway running through Houston. The city was established alongside its shore in 1836.

An **art car** is a special type of "rolling art" that is seen each year during the Houston Art Car Parade and displayed year-round at the Houston Art Car Museum.

Miller Outdoor Theatre offers the most diverse season of professional entertainment of any Houston performance venue, and it's all *free*! Relax in the covered seating area or enjoy a pre-performance picnic on the hillside. All performances at Miller are family-friendly!

The Houston **Texans** are Houston's NFL franchise. To purchase Houston Texans tickets, get more information about the Texans, or become a member of Toro's Kids Club, visit www.HoustonTexans.com.

The Houston **Rockets** are Houston's NBA franchise. To purchase Rockets tickets, become a member of the Rockets Kids Club, or get more information about the Rockets, visit www.Rockets.com.

The Houston Astros® are Houston's MLB franchise, affectionately known as the 'Stros™. To get more information, visit www.Astros.com.

Houston's **Theater District** includes four venues — Jones Hall, Wortham Theatre Center, Alley Theatre and the Hobby Center for the Performing Arts. It is an impressive cultural and entertainment center, featuring seven renowned performing arts organizations, and many smaller ones.

A **wildcatter** is a person who drills for oil in areas not known to be oil fields. The City of Houston grew in large part because of the success of the oil industry.

Each year, The Mayor's Official July 4th Celebration—"Freedom Over Texas"—includes an impressive **fireworks display** as part of the festivities in downtown Houston.

Galveston Bay is a large estuary connected to the Gulf of Mexico about 50 miles south of Houston. Its shores are a favorite spot for those who want to escape the heat of the Houston summer.

Shipley Do-Nuts is a delicious do-nut and pastry chain which began in Houston in the early twentieth century and is now found in Texas, Louisiana, Oklahoma and New Mexico.

House of Pies is a local Houston restaurant that serves up slices of "Heaven on Earth," 24 hours a day.

Space Center Houston is the official visitors' center for the Lyndon B. Johnson Space Center. It is NASA's center for human spaceflight activities, known as the home of mission control and astronaut training. There are many activities for children, including the opportunity to simulate commanding a shuttle and living in space.

The **Houston Arboretum & Nature Center** is a 155-acre sanctuary with five miles of walking trails, located in Houston's beautiful Memorial Park.

The **Downtown Aquarium** in Houston holds a 500,000-gallon aquatic wonderland, with more than 200 species of marine life from around the globe.

The Houston Livestock Show and Rodeo is a 501 (c) (3) charity, supported by more than 24,000 volunteers. It ranks as the world's largest livestock show and rodeo in the world! Started in 1932, the Show has provided more than $250 million in educational support to Texas students.

Artist David Adickes has created 18- to 20-foot tall busts of certain U.S. Presidents which are visible from some of the highways around Houston. You can also see them in Adickes' SculpturWorx Studio in the Heights area of town. They are commonly referred to as the **Presidents' Heads**.

The **Orange Show** is a creation of Houston postman, Jeff McKissack, in honor of his favorite fruit. For 24 years, McKissack used common building materials and found objects to transform an East End lot into an architectural maze of walkways, balconies, arenas and exhibits decorated with mosaics and brightly painted iron figures. The Orange Show site now hosts live performances and the Orange Show Center for Visionary Art runs a number of outreach programs that encourage the public to participate in the creative process. Houston Art Car Weekend is one of its most successful programs.

The **Bluebonnet** is the state flower of Texas. It is Texas tradition to photograph children sitting in fields of bluebonnets.

Discovery Green is a public park in downtown Houston which opened in 2008. It provides a respite from downtown's usual fast pace and hosts many family-friendly activities.

The Houston Galleria Mall includes **Polar Ice Galleria**, an ice skating rink which has been an icon in the Houston area for over 30 years.

The **Gerald D. Hines Waterwall** is a 64-foot tall marvel. This urban waterfall is in the Uptown District.

H-town is a loving nickname given to Houston by its citizens.

Acknowledgements

The authors would like to acknowledge the following:

SONG LYRIC
"The stars at night are big and bright"

Line from:
"Deep in the Heart of Texas"
by June Hershey and Don Swander

Copyright 1941 by
Melody Lane Publications, Inc.

Copyright Renewed.

Used with Permission.

PHOTOGRAPHY
All original photos were used with permission.

Cover
Copyright 2010 Jim Olive
www.stockyard.com

Sam Houston Monument
Alex Wolcott
www.flickr.com/eflon

Hermann Park Railroad
Michael Sweeney

Children's Museum
Henry Yau

Buffalo Bayou
Stanford Moore

Miller Outdoor Theatre
Alma M. Bovara

Art car
Photo by T. Mitchell Jones

Art Car "Faith" created by David Best and part of the Art Car Museum collection.

Minute Maid Park
The Houston Astros®

Major League Baseball trademarks and copyrights are used with permission of Major League Baseball Properties, Inc.

Astronaut
NASA/courtesy of nasaimages.org

Rodeo
Houston Livestock Show and Rodeo

Fireworks display
Photo by Donna Carson

The Mayor's Official July 4th Celebration, "Freedom Over Texas"

Mayor's Office of Special Events file, City of Houston

Orange Show
Tony Frankino

Bluebonnets
Jason E. Heiser

Ice skaters
Jair Alcon
Alconography

Waterwall
Antony Williams
www.flickr.com/photos/antandjo

Houston Skyline with Buffalo Bayou
Copyright Douglas Wilson

A special thank you to all of the institutions, organizations, businesses and individuals who make Houston a great place to live, and whose participation made this book possible.